Animals That Live in the Mountains/
Animales de las montañas

Golden Eagles
Águilas reales

By JoAnn Early Macken

Reading Consultant: Jeanne Clidas, Ph.D.
Director, Roberts Wesleyan College Literacy Clinic

ROCKFORD PUBLIC LIBRARY

Please visit our web site at **www.garethstevens.com**.
For a free catalog describing our list of high-quality books,
call 1-877-542-2595 (USA) or 1-800-387-3178 (Canada).
Our fax: 1-877-542-2596

Library of Congress Cataloging-in-Publication Data

Macken, JoAnn Early, 1953–
    [Golden eagles. Spanish & English]
    Golden eagles = Águilas reales / by JoAnn Early Macken.
       p. cm. — (Animals that live in the mountains = Animales de las montañas)
    Includes bibliographical references and index.
    ISBN-10: 1-4339-2445-5   ISBN-13: 978-1-4339-2445-3 (lib. bdg.)
    ISBN-10: 1-4339-2503-6   ISBN-13: 978-1-4339-2503-0 (soft cover)
    1. Golden eagle—Juvenile literature. I. Title. II. Title: Águilas reales.
QL696.F32M253   2010
98.9'42–dc22   2009007410

This edition first published in 2010 by
Weekly Reader® Books
An Imprint of Gareth Stevens Publishing
1 Reader's Digest Road
Pleasantville, NY 10570-7000 USA

Copyright © 2010 by Gareth Stevens, Inc.

Executive Managing Editor: Lisa M. Herrington
Senior Editor: Barbara Bakowski
Cover Designers: Jennifer Ryder-Talbot and Studio Montage
Production: Studio Montage
Translators: Tatiana Acosta and Guillermo Gutiérrez
Library Consultant: Carl Harvey, Library Media Specialist, Noblesville, Indiana

Photo credits: Cover, pp. 1, 9, 11, 19 Shutterstock; pp. 5, 13, 17 © Tom and Pat Leeson;
p. 7 © Yuri Shibnev/naturepl.com; p. 15 Digital Stock; p. 21 © Alan and Sandy Carey

All rights reserved. No part of this book may be reproduced, stored in a retrieval system,
or transmitted in any form or by any means, electronic, mechanical, photocopying, recording,
or otherwise, without the prior written permission of the copyright holder. For permission, contact
permissions@gspub.com.

Printed in the United States of America

1 2 3 4 5 6 7 8 9 14 13 12 11 10 09

Table of Contents

Baby Eagles 4

Feathers and Flying 8

Strong Hunters 14

Glossary 22

For More Information 23

Index 24

- - - - - - - - - - - - -

Contenido

Crías de águila 4

Plumas y vuelo 8

Grandes cazadoras 14

Glosario 22

Más información 23

Índice 24

Boldface words appear in the glossary./
Las palabras en **negrita** aparecen en el glosario.

Baby Eagles

Golden eagles build huge nests. Each year, they add more sticks. Baby eagles are called **eaglets**. They hatch in the nests.

Crías de águila

Las águilas reales hacen nidos enormes. Cada año añaden nuevos palitos. Las crías de águila se llaman aguiluchos. Los **aguiluchos** salen del huevo en el nido.

An eaglet has soft feathers called **down**. Its father brings it meat to eat. Its mother feeds it small pieces.

- - - - - - - - - - - - - - - -

Un aguilucho tiene unas plumas suaves llamadas **plumón**. Su padre trae carne para alimentarlo. Su madre se la va dando en pequeños trozos.

Feathers and Flying

Eagles start to fly in about three months. They fly and hunt during the day. At night, they rest in trees.

- - - - - - - - - - - - - - -

Plumas y vuelo

Las águilas comienzan a volar, más o menos, a los tres meses. Durante el día, vuelan y cazan. Por la noche, descansan en los árboles.

Golden eagles have gold feathers on their heads and necks. Feathers cover their legs.

- - - - - - - - - - - - - - -

Las águilas reales tienen plumas doradas en la cabeza y el cuello. Sus patas están cubiertas de plumas.

A golden eagle can hear well. It listens for other eagles. It listens for storms. If an eagle gets wet, it may not be able to fly.

- - - - - - - - - - - - - - -

El águila real puede oír muy bien. Oye a otras águilas. Oye la llegada de una tormenta. Si un águila se moja, podría tener problemas para volar.

Strong Hunters

A golden eagle may fly many miles to find food. It can spot **prey** from far away.

Grandes cazadoras

Un águila real puede llegar a volar muchas millas en busca de comida. Es capaz de ver a una **presa** desde muy lejos.

Eagles dive from the sky. They catch their prey with claws called **talons**.

- - - - - - - - - - - - - - -

Las águilas descienden en picado desde el cielo. Atrapan a sus presas con las uñas, o **garras**.

Eagles have strong hooked **beaks**. They tear their prey apart. Golden eagles hunt rabbits and mice. They also eat lizards and birds.

- - - - - - - - - - - - - - -

Las águilas tienen **picos** ganchudos y fuertes. Despedazan a sus presas. Las águilas reales cazan conejos y ratones. También comen lagartos y aves.

In winter, golden eagles may fly to warmer places to find food. They follow their prey down the mountains. In spring, the eagles fly back up.

- - - - - - - - - - - - - - -

En el invierno, las águilas reales pueden volar a lugares más cálidos en busca de comida. Siguen a sus presas a zonas más bajas. En la primavera, las águilas reales regresan a las montañas.

Fast Facts/Datos básicos

Height/ Altura	about 3 feet (1 meter)/ unos 3 pies (1 metro)
Wingspan/ Envergadura	about 7 feet (2 meters)/ unos 7 pies (2 metros)
Weight/ Peso	about 15 pounds (7 kilograms)/ unas 15 libras (7 kilogramos)
Diet/ Dieta	birds and other small animals/aves y otros animales pequeños
Average life span/ Promedio de vida	up to 20 years/ hasta 20 años

Glossary/Glosario

beaks: the bills of birds

down: soft, fluffy feathers

eaglets: baby eagles

prey: animals that are killed for food

talons: claws

---

aguiluchos: crías de águila

garras: uñas afiladas

picos: partes de la cabeza de las aves

plumón: plumas suaves y mullidas

presa: animal devorado por otro animal

For More Information/Más información

Books/Libros

Eagles. New Naturebooks (series). Patrick Merrick (Child's World, 2006)

I Live in the Mountains/Vivo en las montañas. Where I Live (series). Gini Holland (Gareth Stevens, 2004)

Web Sites/Páginas web

Golden Eagle/Águilas reales
www.birds.cornell.edu/AllAboutBirds/BirdGuide/Golden_Eagle_dtl.html
Listen to sound files of an eagle's call./Escuchen cómo suena la llamada de un águila.

Golden Eagle/Águilas reales
www.baldeagleinfo.com/eagle/eagle7.html
Watch a video of a golden eagle./Vean un video de un águila real.

Publisher's note to educators and parents: Our editors have carefully reviewed these web sites to ensure that they are suitable for children. Many web sites change frequently, however, and we cannot guarantee that a site's future contents will continue to meet our high standards of quality and educational value. Be advised that children should be closely supervised whenever they access the Internet.

Nota de la editorial a los padres y educadores: Nuestros editores han revisado con cuidado las páginas web para asegurarse de que son apropiadas para niños. Sin embargo, muchas páginas web cambian con frecuencia, y no podemos garantizar que sus contenidos futuros sigan conservando nuestros elevados estándares de calidad y de interés educativo. Tengan en cuenta que los niños deben ser supervisados atentamente siempre que accedan a Internet.

Index/Índice

beaks 18	food 6, 14, 18, 20	nests 4
diving 16	hearing 12	parents 6
eaglets 4, 6	hunting 8, 14, 16, 18, 20	prey 14, 16, 18, 20
feathers 6, 10	legs 10	talons 16
flying 8, 12, 14, 20		

---

aguiluchos 4, 6	garras 16	picos 18
cazar 8, 14, 16, 18, 20	nidos 4	plumas 6, 10
comida 6, 14, 18, 20	oído 12	presas 14, 16, 18, 20
descenso en picado 16	padres 6	volar 8, 12, 14, 20
	patas 10	

About the Author

JoAnn Early Macken is the author of two rhyming picture books, *Sing-Along Song* and *Cats on Judy*, and more than 80 nonfiction books for children. Her poems have appeared in several children's magazines. She lives in Wisconsin with her husband and their two sons.

Información sobre la autora

JoAnn Early Macken ha escrito dos libros de rimas con ilustraciones, *Sing-Along Song* y *Cats on Judy*, y más de ochenta libros de no ficción para niños. Sus poemas han sido publicados en varias revistas infantiles. Vive en Wisconsin con su esposo y sus dos hijos.

ROCKFORD PUBLIC LIBRARY

3 1112 018046363

SPA J 598.942 MAC
Macken, JoAnn Early
aAguilas reales = Golden
eagles

092910

ROCKFORD PUBLIC LIBRARY

Rockford, Illinois

www.rockfordpubliclibrary.org

815-965-9511